ooh la la!
perfect face

ooh la la!
perfect face

Susie Galvez

Illustrated by Chico Hayasaki

MQP

Published by MQ Publications Limited
12 The Ivories
6–8 Northampton Street
London, N1 2HY
email: mail@mqpublications.com
website: www.mqpublications.com

Copyright © MQ Publications Limited 2004
Text copyright © Susie Galvez 2004

Illustrator: Chico Hayasaki/www.cwc-i.com
Editor: Laura Kesner
Senior Designer: Victoria Bevan

ISBN: 1-84072-590-7
10 9 8 7 6 5 4 3 2 1

This book is intended as an informational guide only and is not to be used as a substitute
for professional medical care or treatment. Neither the author nor the publisher can be
held responsible for any damage, injury, or otherwise resulting from the use of the
information in this book.

Printed and bound in France by *Partenaires-Livres*® (JL)

Contents

Introduction

Let's face it, your face is your calling card. The world forms hundreds of assumptions about you based simply on the color, shape, and size of your facial features.

Ooh La La! Perfect Face gets up close and personal with 101 tips that will create a dramatic difference in the statement your face makes. Learn about long-term strategies for keeping your skin looking its best. Keep it clean with deep-down dirt fighters. Banish skin problems with homemade remedies for soothing and smoothing. Find out what to stock in your handbag to fix facial beauty emergencies—pronto!

From skin care secrets to flash fixes, it's all here in *Ooh La La! Perfect Face*.

So, the next time you meet someone for the first time, smile—and put your best face forward!

Chapter 1
Beauty emergencies

Zits happen

When you least expect it, an eruption of the worst kind appears out of nowhere on your face. No time to think about what caused it, your immediate goal is to get rid of it or hide it fast! First, wash the perpetrator with an anti-bacterial cleanser. This will prevent the pesky zit from spreading to other facial areas. Next, put a dab of oil-free moisturizer on the afflicted area. Finally, dab on a yellow-based corrector with a foundation sponge and wait at least two minutes before patting the area with a yellow-toned powder. The zit is now hidden from view. Upon removing the day's makeup, be sure to cleanse the area with anti-bacterial soap and put a drying lotion on the bump. With a little luck, the zit will just be a memory by morning!

It is a good idea to change pillowcases often. As you toss and turn during the night, hair products come off on the pillowcase. In turn, this nasty residue is then transferred to your facial skin. Fabric softener may also aggravate skin, as the ingredients that make clothes less clingy coat the pillow fabric and are transferred to your face as you sleep. Make it a habit to change pillowcases at least once or twice a week, and avoid using fabric softener on materials that will come into contact with your face.

About face

If your face is prone to breakouts in certain areas, here are some possible culprits. Breakouts located on the side of the face may indicate the use of a dirty telephone receiver—check your phone now. Pimples along the forehead might be from oil buildup on the bangs or from hairstyling products. Chin bumps could simply be the result of good old Mother Nature's hormones, as this is the area that usually acts up monthly. Breakouts could also occur if you rest your hands on your chin excessively. Hands carry a lot of grime that can be transferred to your face.

Hot and cold

For a quick pick-me-up, whatever the weather, either cool it down or turn up the heat. In warm weather, keep cleansing gels, lotions, and creams in the refrigerator. The cool, crisp feeling you get when using them will revive a hot, tired face. During colder months, begin the cleansing process by placing a warm, wet washcloth over your entire face to gently warm it up. Also, take a minute to warm products in your hands before applying them to the face or body. This will take off the cold edge and will allow the products to absorb more deeply into the skin.

Pimple potion

If a sudden eruption has you running for cover—try these sure-fire cures.

* Take a mixture of one tablespoon of water and one tablespoon of salt
  and place on the pimple. Do not rub. Allow to dry and rinse off.
  Apply twice a day until bump is gone.

* Soak a cotton ball in milk, squeeze excess,
  place on the bump, and leave for
  15 minutes.

* A bit of toothpaste on a pimple
  works wonders. Before going to bed,
  put a small dab on the eruption and
  allow it to remain overnight.

Pick a remedy that works for you. Try them
all, as different bumps call for different cures.

Strike oil

If lack of sleep or over-indulging in food or drink has your face looking like a close-up of the desert—strike oil! On a night when you are staying in, cleanse your face. Mix together two tablespoons of olive oil or evening primrose oil with one tiny drop of tea tree oil. Mix together and apply to the face, neck and décolleté. Massage until most of the oil has penetrated. Put a towel over your pillow to protect it and lie down for 15 minutes. When time is up, gently massage any non-absorbed oils into the skin. Get a good night's rest and awaken with a new face the next day!

Lip appeal

To get rid of dry, cracked lips, put a tiny bit of petroleum jelly on them and rub gently with an old toothbrush. Open a vitamin E gel capsule and rub the gel over the surface of the lips. (Apply any leftover vitamin E oil to the fingernail cuticles for extra hydration.) Wait for five minutes and then rub a small drop of olive oil on the lips to help seal in the moisture.

Ice, ice, baby

If your skin is screaming, "I'm sensitive," "I'm chapped," "I'm irritated," here is the perfect cure. Make a pot of chamomile tea. Cool and pour into an ice cube tray. Freeze. Take out a frozen cube, wrap in cotton gauze, and rub gently around the face for five minutes. Then take a cotton ball soaked in milk and press over the entire facial area for five minutes. The skin will be calm and de-stressed. This treatment is also excellent for post-waxing sensitivities.

Masquerade

To mask a blemish quickly, mix a drop of witch hazel and a bit of your foundation together. This will turn any foundation into a medicated one. Witch hazel contains anti-bacterial properties to help prevent the spread of bacteria, as well as soothing ingredients that will aid in healing. For best results apply with a clean makeup sponge, and be sure to dab a little extra on the blemish. You will be both treating the blemish and covering the culprit.

Taking cover

To treat a troublesome, ongoing blemish, try using a medicated blemish product. There are several on the market from clear products, to ones that contain foundation color to help camouflage as well as treat—choose the one that best suits your needs. The ingredients are designed to dry the pimple up fast. Because this effective product can be quite drying, only apply directly to the blemish. Try to avoid any surrounding skin, since contact will cause flakiness on healthy skin.

Frequent flyer

Air on long airplane flights can be dehydrating to your skin, and contrary to popular belief, drinking water doesn't suffice. (You will have already landed by the time it has any positive effect—but please do it anyway!) In addition to drinking extra water, at the flight's mid-point, wash your face and rehydrate the skin. Your skin will look and feel better and it is a great flight reviver for those trans-continental trips.

Take five

It only takes five minutes to refresh your face. Even in our warp speed world, you should always allow yourself time to improve your skin. First, wash your face with your favorite cleanser. Then apply a hydrating, deeply penetrating mask. Leave on for four to five minutes. Rinse with warm water and put on a vitamin-rich moisturizer. There, now don't you feel (and look) better?

Unmasked

If there is one skin care product that can work immediate miracles, it is a face mask. Skin changes with the seasons, so be sure to take into consideration the elements outside when choosing a mask.

While dry skins are renewed with a moisture-enhanced mask, oily skins greatly benefit from clay and mud types of masks. Some even contain exfoliating ingredients so that the dead, dry, skin cells can be better whisked away along with the mask when it is removed. For combination skins, do as the pros do

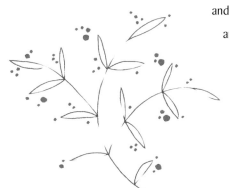

and use a dry skin mask for the cheeks, and an oily mask for oily areas such as forehead, nose, and chin. Don't forget your neck—it needs reviving too!

Get misty

To keep skin hydrated, keep a spritzer of mineral water or rose water on hand to mist away the environment. Climate-controlled buildings, cars, and homes create air that is devoid of moisture, leaving the skin's surface parched. Add a little mist to your life to refresh, rehydrate, and make you feel good.

A little dab will do you

Keep a tiny tube or jar of moisturizer in your makeup bag. If your skin begins to feel dry or taut, especially around the eye area or upper lip, use the ring finger to tap a little bit of cream onto the area. Dryness will disappear and smoothness will return to the skin.

The puffy police

If you look in the mirror and all you see are puffy, puffy, puffy eyes, rescue is on the way. Apply two brewed, cooled, caffeinated tea bags to the eye area and lie down. Allow the caffeine in the tea bags to gently pull excess water from the area. This treatment is also good for dark circles.

Cucumbers also work well. Cut two medium slices of cucumber and place over the eye area. The cucumber hydrates and purifies the area, allowing the excess fluids to drain safely away from the eyes.

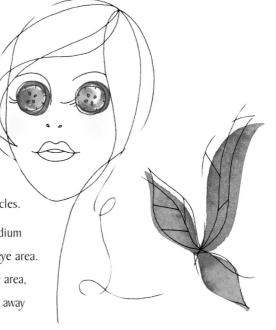

Eye, eye, captain

Red, bloodshot eyes are caused by the swelling of the tiny blood vessels on the eye's surface, which can be caused by lack of sleep, excessive time spent in front of a computer, a smoke-filled environment, or an infection. If it is a persistent problem, consult your doctor. On a temporary basis, you can use eyedrops to bring the sparkle back to your eyes. These contain ingredients to reduce the swelling in the blood vessels and will decrease redness as well as cutting down on dryness and irritability.

Unpack your bags

Eye bags or eye puffiness are a fact of life for some of us. Maybe we have eaten the wrong foods, indulged in too much alcohol, or maybe we are just born with them. Whatever the reason— we want to send them packing!

To force the packed bags out of town, try physical exercise. Walking or jogging for 15 minutes is often enough to drain the excess fluid out from under the eyes. If that is out of the question, try walking on the spot or going up and down the stairs for ten minutes to encourage the fluid to get on its way.

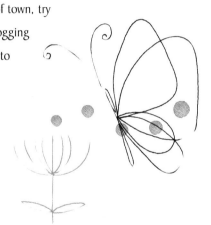

Sea sure

What if, dear heavens, while at the office or away from home, a sudden breakout occurs and all of your trusty blemish-bashing potions are sitting on your dressing table? Simply take the sea cure. Take four ounces of warm water, add one tablespoon of table salt, and mix well. Dip a cotton ball or a facial tissue in the solution and apply to the bump. Keep the pad in place for two to three minutes. Repeat with a new cotton ball or facial tissue. Leave longer if desired and then pat dry. This treatment should knock the wind out of the blemish's sails.

X marks the spot

To determine if your skin is really sensitive or not, use this x-cellent tip. With a clean thumbnail, gently make an "X" between your eyebrows. If the redness remains for a while, your skin is sensitive in addition to your usual skin type (i.e. normal/sensitive, oily/sensitive, etc.). Now you finally know what you thought all along!

Cold sore no more

If a cold sore suddenly comes on the scene, ice it. Putting ice on the beginnings of a cold sore lowers the skin's metabolic rate and stops the cold sore from turning over as quickly. Another way to take the bite out of a cold sore is to bathe the blister in three percent hydrogen peroxide or rubbing alcohol. Place either the three percent hydrogen peroxide or rubbing alcohol on a cotton ball and hold against the cold sore, pressing

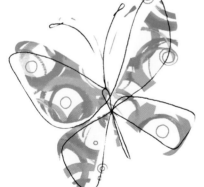

lightly. *Note:* please do not try this method if the skin is broken.

Afterward, allow a wet, previously steamed tea bag to cool, and place on the area for five minutes. The tannic acid in the tea bag will reduce a cold sore's inflammation.

Bedside manner

Lips have no way to moisturize themselves as they contain no oil glands. Lips can, and do, dry out during the night, especially if you breathe through your mouth while sleeping, or if the bedroom is warm and dry. To keep lips soft and kissable, nourish them nocturnally.

Get in the habit of keeping a moisturizing, vitamin-enriched lip balm on your nightstand. Apply to the entire lip area before you go to bed to keep the lips moist and hydrated. When you toss and turn, take an extra moment, and reach for your lip conditioner to condition and moisturize the lips as you lull yourself back to sleep.

Chapter 2

More than skin deep

Deep down

Beauty starts on the inside and radiates to the outside. If you are "Livin' La Vida Loca" like the rest of us, then you should kick start that inner beauty with a good daily vitamin supplement! Since many foods are now overly processed and devoid of the vitamins that our skin needs, getting all of

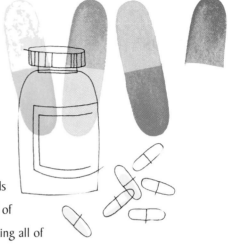

the necessary nutrients from food is unlikely to happen. You should take a daily multi-vitamin to ensure your skin gets what it needs to be beautiful. Find a good multi-vitamin with at least 100 percent of the daily recommended requirements. Take your vitamins with your breakfast meal, as the nutrients are better released with food. If you decide to take other skin-enhancing supplements, even better. Keep on top of what is deep down.

Holding back the years

Antioxidants are one of the best ways to keep the signs of aging at bay.
An easy way to increase your antioxidant intake is by drinking herbal teas.
If you are a regular coffee or tea drinker, start replacing one cup of these
dehydrating beverages with healthy, antioxidant-laden herbal tea. Lemon
balm, peppermint, spearmint, and green tea are significant sources of
age-defying antioxidants. Did I hear someone say "tea time"?

Calm down

Green tea is a natural anti-inflammatory that reduces redness and calms
irritated skin. When skin is on the edge, steep a green tea bag in a teacup
for seven minutes, allowing all of the green tea's goodness to distill. Pour onto
a washcloth, squeeze slightly, and place over the entire face. Relax for ten to
15 minutes, re-soak the cloth, and relax for an additional five minutes. Pat dry.
Add moisture and allow skin to rest. This treatment can be done daily until
skin calmness returns.

"C" the illumination

If it's that radiant, lit-from-within glow you crave, look no further than vitamin C. Its capillary-strengthening abilities help to transport nutrients to the skin's upper layers, fighting the appearance of tiny spider veins and rosacea. It also ensures that the blood supply stays close to the skin's surface, giving skin a pink, rosy bloom. Vitamin C is found in citrus fruits, guavas, kiwifruits, mangoes, papayas, peaches, and strawberries.

Double duty

Studies show that a daily diet rich in raw vegetables and fruits tends to make the skin more radiant and the eyes brighter, as none of the nutrients are lost during cooking. Add a couple of raw carrots, cauliflower, broccoli, apples, or celery to your food plan for optimum skin (and diet!) results.

Hey! Can you hear me?

Here is the number one beauty tip in the world—
DRINK WATER. There is nothing that makes a
bigger difference to your beauty life than water—
period. Water flushes toxins from the body,
hydrates the skin, and keeps things moving
along. If you are not drinking eight glasses of
this beauty product each and every day, you
are literally starving your cells. If you are not
drinking enough water, don't bother with other
beauty products—you are just throwing your
money and your face away. Sipper cups anyone?!

   Perfect Face

An ounce of prevention

If your breakouts are stress related, this tip could help reduce breakouts before a stressful event. Prior to retiring the night before the stressful event, chew two antacid tablets. Excess acid from the heightened stress level is typically the problem. Taking the tablet the night before will calm the acids before they begin.

Get it together

Keeping all of your skin care products in one place will help you to complete your daily skin care regime with ease. A large wicker basket on your countertop or under your cabinet is the perfect place to store all of your beauty products. The neat, clean look of the countertop soothes your senses as you get ready to start or end your day.

Feeding your face

Your skin needs the right nutrients to make new skin cells. Just applying products to the skin will not do it—you need much more than that. All the vitamins in the world, topically applied, cannot make up for a face that is lacking in a healthy diet program, devoid of nutritious, and good-for-you, foods. Feed your cells from the inside out.

By eating a diet rich with fresh foods like fruit and vegetables, brown rice, whole-wheat bread, grilled chicken and fish, and low fat cheeses and yogurts, you will help the skin glow. Eating correctly is important to the look of your skin, so remember to try and include at least some of the foods listed above in your daily diet.

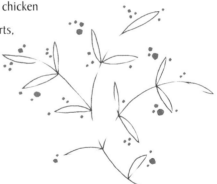

Off the vine

Try to eat five portions of fruit or vegetables a day in order to improve the condition of your skin. It is easy to add skin-saving and enhancing nutrients to your diet—at lunchtime, simply add some carrot, sprigs of broccoli, cauliflower, or celery to your salad. At breakfast time, drop a couple of slices of banana or apple onto your cereal to gain the most of what nature's bounty has to offer. Drinking a smoothie on the run is a quick and easy way to fill up on goodness. A few additions to your diet every week is all that it takes to enjoy the health benefits—helping you to live longer, prosper, and look more beautiful at the same time!

Smoke alarm

This can't be the first place that you have learned that smoking is bad for you. But maybe, just maybe, since you are reading a book about perfect faces, you will give it up for beauty.

Smoking makes you look old before your time as nicotine constricts the small blood vessels and decreases the flow of oxygen and nutrients to the skin. The area first affected is the lips— a smoker's lip line—not pretty! For goodness sake, there is NOTHING good about smoking. Give it up!

What's up doc?

Raw vegetable juices contain vital vitamins, minerals, and enzymes, which can be absorbed into the bloodstream in less than 20 minutes. Drink the juice straightaway to prevent oxidation from leaching out some of the wonderful nutrients.

Carrot juice is at the top of your skin's wish list. Rich in vitamins A, B, C, D, and E, one glass will boost your immune system, fight infection, and protect against digestive disorders.

Cell-a-brate

True beauty is never just skin deep. Beauty comes from deep inside the soul and radiates through each cell. Make sure you are eating the right kinds of food, and drinking enough water, so that the healthy cells inside your body show on the outside.

S.O.S.

Save our skin. Did you know that up to 25 percent of valuable vitamins, minerals, and fiber in fruit and vegetables might be lost in the process of peeling? Given the opportunity, don't peel, just wash thoroughly. One good way to ensure that fruit and vegetables are squeaky clean is to use a vegetable brush with a bit of anti-bacterial soap and gently scrub the fruit or vegetable's outer peel. Rinse with cool water and wipe dry with a paper towel. To gain the most nutrients from green, leafy vegetables, instead of tossing out the outermost leaves of lettuce, cabbage, and spinach, which contain the highest vitamin and mineral content, how about giving them a bath? Fill a large bowl or the sink with cool water and a tiny bit of anti-bacterial soap. Allow to soak for a few minutes and then rinse well. Dry the leaves on a paper towel, or spin dry in a vegetable spinner. Clean as a whistle and now even more good for your face!

Plump it up

Healthy skin equals plump skin. Essential fatty acids (EFAs) are important allies when it comes to skin health. Skin that has a dry, grayish look is a sign of a diet poor in EFAs. EFAs are "good fats"—to be sure that you are getting enough of them in your diet, make it a habit to include weekly servings of oily fish, such as mackerel, herring, sardines, fresh tuna, trout, and salmon. Nuts, sunflower seeds, and sunflower oil are also an excellent way to get your fair share of EFAs—serve over salads for a skin-plumping treat.

Siesta time

Did you realize that losing just one hour of sleep a night for a week equals seven hours—or one whole night? As you can imagine, these lost hours show up first on the face. Lack of sleep may also lead to increased itching or burning eyes, blurred vision, headaches, or feeling chilled, as well as waves of sleepiness or fatigue, irritability, weepiness, and short-term memory loss. Not a pretty picture. The quickest way back into the sleep vault is to bank a few naps. Sleep in on the weekends when you have the opportunity. Take an afternoon siesta, close your door and your eyes for 30 minutes to one hour. You will awaken feeling refreshed, revived, and raring to go.

Wake up and smell the coffee

The chemicals responsible for java's signature scent have powerful antioxidant properties. To maximize their benefits, chug your cup of Joe within 20 minutes of brewing.

Perfect Face

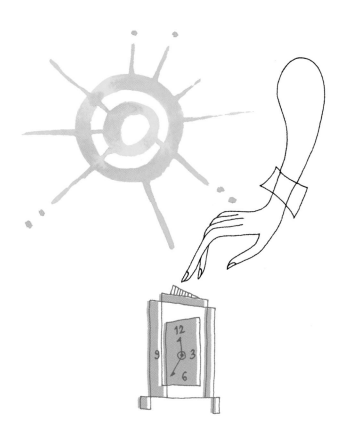

Get the lead out

Silver or metal fillings in your teeth scream "out of date." Make an appointment with your dentist to remove the amalgam fillings and replace with composite (plastic and ceramic) or porcelain. When you laugh, all that will be exposed is a great laugh and not a silver mine in your mouth!

In the middle of the night

Taking evening primrose oil and vitamin E capsules before retiring allows the body to absorb these powerful anti-agers into the system during its most restorative time. Take the rest of your vitamins in the morning after your breakfast, but retain these two skin-saving vitamins until bedtime for the best results.

In the shade

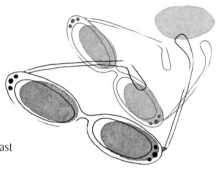

Sunglasses are not an option, they are an anti-aging necessity. The eyes are the first place to show signs of aging. If you are squinting or exposing the sensitive eye area to excessive sunlight, you are on the fast track to aging.

Protect your windows to the soul by choosing sunglasses with 100 percent UVA and UVB ray absorption. Plastics are the best choice for frames and lenses since they will not break and are less permeable to UV rays. Plus, plastic is a lot lighter to wear.

Be sure to keep any parts that touch the skin clean to avoid breakouts. Areas to monitor are the earpieces, the bridge of the nose, and the cheeks, if the glass frame rests there. Clean with a cotton ball soaked in a bit of facial toner and water. Gently wipe areas clean at least once a week, and more often on vacation where sunglass usage is usually increased.

Chapter 3

The long term

Sleep tight

We have talked about not getting enough sleep and all of the physical symptoms that it can cause, but did you know that lack of sleep also inhibits the immune system's ability to fight off viruses and bacteria. You may not be aware that viruses and bacteria can cause pimples and acne. As we sleep, our entire body is going about the business of repairing itself. Our skin does most of its repairs between the hours of 1 A.M. and 4 A.M. Lack of sleep during this cell rejuvenating time can trigger stress that causes the skin to look dull, tired, puffy, or sallow. Even worse—breakouts of pimples or acne could suddenly appear! Getting enough sleep is critical to your mental and physical health—not to mention the effect that lack of sleep has on the condition of your skin. Remember, it is called "beauty sleep," so get your daily dose of beauty—starting tonight!

Say nope to soap

The best way to cleanse the face is with a cleanser designed especially for the face. Leave the soap for areas below the décolleté. If you love the clean, fresh feeling of suds and water, then a rinse-off cleanser is the perfect way to rid the face of dirt, oils, and makeup. Tissue-off products have a tendency to pull the skin, and can leave residue and oil on the face since they are not washed off. Keep the fresh feeling that washing brings by using wash-off cleansers and saying nope to soap. Remember, the face is the only part of the body that is always exposed. Only expose it to products that are effective yet gentle.

Peaks and valleys

Lines can look worse than they really are if excessive dead skin is allowed to remain on the skin's surface. When too many extra cells are left on the skin, light catches the lines and makes them more pronounced, as well as making pores look larger. By removing extra dead skin cells via manual, chemical, or machine exfoliation, lines appear less noticeable. Remove the peaks—lessen the valleys. Plan a good exfoliation session soon!

Some things are not negotiable

Moisturizing is a must. Skin of all ages demands the use of a moisturizer. Be it oil-free lotion, or cream laden with dry-skin-fighting oils. Choose the perfect formula for your skin type and use it daily. A moisturizer's job is to create a protection field against the environment. You want to keep the good stuff in and the bad stuff out and off the face!

Snow patrol

If you spend a lot of time outside, engaged in winter sports like skiing or skating, be cautious when using water-based products. They can actually freeze on your face causing windburn-like redness. Oil-based moisturizers and foundations have a higher freezing point and are best for colder climates and conditions. If your plans include outside activities, remember to modify your daily beauty routine. Even oily skins will be okay with the oil-based moisturizer, if kept to short usages.

Facial smoothie

A fast skin-picker-upper is to blend a facial smoothie. Place $\frac{1}{4}$ cup of melon, $\frac{1}{4}$ cup of fresh pineapple, and $\frac{1}{2}$ cup of seltzer water in a blender. Mix well. Apply the mixture to the face and neck, and allow the mask to remain on the skin for 15 minutes. Rinse well with cold water to tighten your pores, pat dry, and apply moisturizer to finish the treatment. Pineapple contains enzymes that help remove dead skin cells, while the melon gently moisturizes and rehydrates your face. The seltzer water adds a little effervescence to help speed up the action of the fruit combo and to make it work more effectively.

Facial expressions

An esthetician, or facialist, is a professional who has had specific training on the care, wellness, problems, and conditions of the skin. Part of the training includes being able to diagnose skin ailments and suggest regimes to heal them. A good facial should include thorough cleaning, toning, exfoliating, steaming, and massaging of the skin, as well as a mask suited for individual skin conditions and moisturization of the facial and eye areas. Once you find a good esthetician, your skin troubles are virtually over. It is worth the search.

Caught on tape

If you suspect your skin care regime is missing the mark, take the tape test. On a day when you are makeup free, after having your moisturizer on for at least two hours, put a small strip of adhesive tape on the areas of the face near the jawbone and lower cheek area and gently lift it off. If the tape surface is full of your face surface, such as dry skin cells and debris, your regime is not working. You need to uncover another kind of moisturizer—pronto!

Nitty gritty

Facial scrubs help remove dead skin cells and surface grime, leaving the skin feeling firm and smooth. Facial buffing pads and brushes are too abrasive—even though they are sold as a "facial" item.

Choose a facial scrub with tiny granules that dissolve in water. Use the scrub once or twice a week, depending on your skin type. To use, wash your face and apply a small amount of facial scrub to face and neck while the face is still wet from rinsing. Rinse well and apply your moisturizer.

You can even make your own scrub. Choose from the list below:

✳ Combine two tablespoons of grapefruit juice and two tablespoons of uncooked oatmeal, apply in gentle circular motions and rinse well.

✳ Add one teaspoon of granulated sugar to your regular facial cleanser, apply to face and neck and rinse well.

✳ Combine two tablespoons of ground almonds with two tablespoons of olive oil, apply in gentle circular motions and rinse well.

One step forward

Radiant skin requires a healthy diet, lots of water, exercise, and plenty of rest. Smoking, excess sun exposure, and too much alcohol are menaces to the skin, causing lines and wrinkles, and discoloration. All the cleansers, creams, peels, and even face-lifts in the world are all for naught if you are not living a healthy lifestyle. If you have postponed dropping a poor habit, now is the time to put the plan in motion. Start today and plan a beautiful life.

Now that's culture

Plain yogurt is an excellent facial mask—just as it is. First, cleanse
the face and neck thoroughly, then open the container and apply the
contents to your face, neck, and, for an even better treatment,
apply to your décolleté as well. Relax and lie down
for 15 minutes. The plain yogurt contains lactic
acid, which works as a natural exfoliator, while milk
proteins gently moisturize the skin.

Facial facts

Did you know that our hard-working skin renews itself about every three to four
weeks (depending on our age)? And that we lose about 30 pounds of dead skin cells
in our lifetime? To further this thought process, when you look around and see things
that need dusting—realize that 80 percent of the dust is actually dead skin cells.

The skin has a tough job, that's for sure. You can make the job easier by doing
your part both inside and out!

Begin where you are

Even if you have never taken proper care of you skin, start now! If you begin now and incorporate a two-minute skin care regime in the morning and again in the evening, you can combat the aging process. The only way an anti-aging treatment works is if you remember to use it—every single day! Begin today. Start cleansing, toning, and hydrating your skin today, tomorrow, and all of the tomorrows after!

Cash in your chips

Even if you cannot go for a facial as much as you would like, plan on moving funds around to have at least two—one at the end of winter and one at the end of summer. When the seasons change dramatically, the skin goes through a lot of changes as well. A good, professional facial will remove the season from your face. It will take off the extra dead skin cells that these seasons bring, as well as prepare the skin for a new day.

An oldie but a goodie

Just because a skin treatment is not the newest product on the shelf or the latest technology, it does not mean it is not the best for your particular skin condition. While the skin care industry is continually formulating new products and defining what works well on the skin and what is no longer as effective, individual judgment needs to be used. Old skin care treatments aren't necessarily ineffective; they are still around because they have remained firm favorites with the buying public— probably because they still continue to work! The same is often true of new-fangled skin treatments. A big trend at the moment in spa facial treatments is using microcurrents to stimulate collagen and elastin growth in the skin. The treatment and its philosophy have actually been around since the 1930s, but it is only now gaining in popularity. It's interesting to keep up with the latest trends, but don't get carried away—remember the tried and true.

AHA aha!

Did you know that most alpha hydroxy acid products (AHAs) contain moisturizers in the formula? Depending on the product's composition, you may only need one product to both exfoliate and hydrate. Read the label and ask a skin care consultant which formula would be best for your skin care needs.

Not always as nature intended

Just because a product says it is natural does not mean it is good for us. Poison ivy is natural, but you would never think of putting it on your skin or brewing it for your afternoon tea. Chemicals can help products last longer, keep them bacteria free, and aid in further penetration of "natural" ingredients.

The best products are a blend of science and nature, working in perfect harmony. Think wisely when choosing the best products for your individual skin type.

The incredible shrinking woman

If your skin feels tight and squeaky clean after cleansing and toning, you have probably just shrunk it! The taut feeling is caused by the over-removal of all hydration, thus causing the skin to shrink. Switch your cleansing products pronto! Choose a cleanser and toner that leave your skin clean without stripping it. You want to be able to smile without cracking up! Being truly confident is knowing that you look and feel great in your own skin. What a wonderful feeling!

Who's calling

Be careful where you put your face. Telephone receivers, both ear and mouthpiece, continually rub against the skin, piling on bacteria and old makeup, as well as grime from your hands. If you notice breakouts on the chin, cheeks, or up near the ears—the phone has got your number!

Clean the phone regularly and make it a habit to keep your hands off your face. Remind yourself not to prop. Hands pick up all kinds of grime. Yuk!

Now I lay me down

Going to bed wearing makeup takes at least ten days off the life of your face. Tossing and turning grinds makeup into the pores and causes grime to go deeper. The eyelashes also take a terrible beating by being squished with dried, cakey mascara, which causes them to break off. Just two minutes is all that it takes to take the day off your face and prepare your skin for a good night—and an excellent skin life!

Chapter 4

Up close
and personal

Brow wow

Although brow styles change as often as fashion trends, opt out on the trends. Find a brow style that suits your face and your eye shape, and keep up with the maintenance. If you simply must have a new shape to your brow other than the one nature intended, do not, I repeat, do not attempt this at home. Brow hair is the most unpredictable hair on the body. It may not grow back if you overdo it on the removal.

Avoid disaster. Allow a professional to shape your brows. Professionals can see the entire facial shape, not just the brows. They can see how your hair grows and can easily fix unruly brows and wild hairs. Creating a sleek shape that totally flatters your face takes time, and most importantly, skill. After shaping, ask how you can maintain the look between waxing or tweezing sessions.

Fast frame

If you have not changed your eyeglasses frame style in more than two years, you need to update your look. You may have the latest hairdo, makeup techniques, and even the most fashion-forward clothes, but if your eyeglasses are yesterday's news, so is your look. Glasses are now an accessory, just like jewelry. Invest in 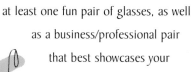 at least one fun pair of glasses, as well as a business/professional pair that best showcases your eyes, your hair, your face, and your total look. To look your best, invest— in yourself.

Tweeze squeeze

If tweezing is uncomfortably painful, try desensitizing the area first. Numb the area with a small bit of aspirin cream. Another good "pain reliever" is to apply a drop of a tooth anesthetic such as Anbesol before beginning the tweezing session.

Brow how

The best time to tweeze is after you have showered. Steam from the shower helps open the pores, allowing for easier removal. The worst time to tweeze is during your monthly cycle, since skin is more tender, or when you are tired, as the tendency is to overdo and remove too much. As you have heard, brow hair is quite unpredictable and may or may not grow back after tweezing. Plan to keep tweezing on the light side.

Sealed with a kiss

It turns out that lip prints are as individual as our fingerprints. No two lip prints are ever the same. So when you decide to "kiss off" and leave your mark—it really will be your very own personal print. Enjoy your special brand of individualism! Next time you go to check out the latest in lip colors at your favorite makeup place, ask the consultant how best to create your very own individual lip style. Perhaps your lips sport a pout, or maybe the perfect bow on top—whatever statement your lips are making, ask the consultant to show you how to show off your individuality.

Eye see

When applying eye cream, be sure to apply to the entire outer eye area, from the under eye socket outward to the area touching the temple, and up around the brow line. Pay extra attention to the laugh lines. To see where extra care is needed, squint your eyes and notice how far the lines extend. To keep any extra lines away, be sure to include all areas with every application.

The future is so bright

Wear your sunglasses! Sunglasses protect our eyes from harmful UVA and UVB sunrays. Eye protection is not only important to keep the wrinkles away from our peepers, but overexposing our eyes can also cause inflammation of the cornea and even cataracts!

If you live in, or travel to a very hot climate, be sure to look for sunglass lenses with infrared protection to keep your eyes cool and comfortable.

Paper trail

If you are unsure whether your moisturizer, foundation, or sunscreen is truly oil-free, put it on paper. Put a dab of the questionable product on a piece of sturdy stationery and allow it to sit for a day. Pick it up and hold the paper to the light. Check for rings around any of the blobs of product you placed there. See a ring? It is not oil-free!

Numbers game

In regard to the look of your face, it is all in the numbers. At the age of 20 you have the skin that you are born with. At 40 you have the skin that you purchased via skincare and cosmetic products. And—either way—at 60 you have the skin that you deserve! Add the numbers up for yourself!

Beauty buster

Bad breath knocks the wind out of beauty. Bad breath can be caused by many factors, including food, drink, diet, hygiene, or health. It is very difficult to smell your own breath to test if it is less than fresh. The only sure way— other than asking a good friend to tell you—is to take the matter into your own hands.

Bad breath can sometimes be detected by licking the inside palm of your hand. Allow it to dry for about 30 seconds and smell the area that you licked. If the beauty breath bouquet has begun to wither, remedy quick with a sugar-free breath mint.

Avoid the curiously strong kinds that are on the market because they contain sugar. Sugar will only mask the problem until the mint dissolves—then because of the sugar, bad breath is back.

Crack a smile

A smile instantly melts the heart and lifts years from your face. A dazzling smile begins and ends with sparkling teeth. Teeth are very vulnerable to staining— from red wine, tea, coffee, and some foods like berries. Brushing regularly for a minimum of two minutes a day is a must. If stains persist, consider a professional whitening treatment available at your dentist's office. After the dentist removes the stains, a simple home-care plan will keep your smile bright and razzle-dazzling.

Behind the scenes

Skin type is of the utmost importance in determining a proper skincare regime. To best determine your personal skin type, count on the professionals. Have a skin analysis, and if possible, have it performed under a skin scanner. This will determine exactly what type of skin you have; it sees your skin literally under the surface. The ultraviolet light will be able to pick up sun-damaged areas, white and blackheads, oil production, and dry areas—even before they are seen by the naked eye. Once the skin has been scanned, a program can be prescribed to offset and prevent any further damage.

Peeper keeper

You should plan on seeing your eye doctor at least once every two years—more often if you have eye problems. The visit will help ensure that the windows to your soul are sound and problem-free. With the amount of rubbing, crying, putting makeup on and taking it off, reading, working in front of a computer screen, sun, wind, cold, and heat our eyes are regularly subjected to—a checkup is probably just what the doctor ordered!

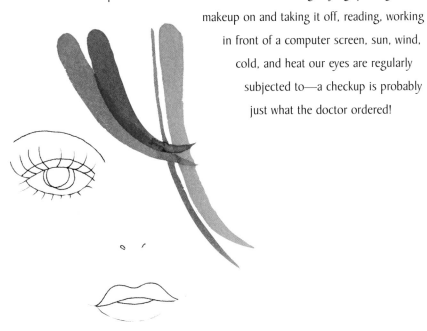

Perfect Face

Eye like it simple

If using eyedrops is a daily habit for you, avoid those with any extra ingredients—especially the "red out" formulas. Constantly using a "red out" formula of eyedrops has been shown to make the problem continue, as the eyes become dependent on the "red out" ingredient. Opt for a formula as close to natural tears as possible. The eye will be refreshed without any extra, irritating side effects.

Taking the redeye

Working at a computer for long periods of time can result in red eyes. Computers create static that attracts dust from the atmosphere and draws it right past your eyes and onto the computer screen. One only has to rub a finger on the screen to see the dirt and grime!

To reduce the red-eye-causing dust and dirt in the air, place an ionizer in your home or office-space. The ionizer will pull dirt in and trap it, leaving your computer screen—and your eyes—cleaner and brighter!

Water works

It is not news that we need to drink at least eight, eight-ounce glasses of water each and every day of our lives. But a lot of people don't know why we need so much. First, water is responsible for about $\frac{1}{2}$ of our body's content—our brains alone contain 75 percent of this life-affirming liquid.

Water is also essential for keeping our digestive system working properly, eliminating toxins, lubricating our joints and eyes, keeping skin supple, and helping to protect our nervous system.

In addition, water is the key element in keeping our bodies in shape. It suppresses the appetite and helps the liver and kidneys to function well.

If you only drink when you feel the thirst urge, you are like a duck out of water. The sensation of thirst is not triggered until there is already a water deficit, so drink before you get thirsty to keep your body's system humming a happy tune.

Forget the frown

Frownies have been used by beautiful women to lessen the look of lines along the forehead since the late 1800s. These are small, skin-colored adhesive papers that you stick onto the forehead so that you cannot frown. Used regularly, they really do help frowns to disappear and they make the forehead appear smoother.

Quick draw

To help capture the perfect eyebrow line, first try drawing on your eyebrows. Use a brow pencil to draw on your ideal shape, then pluck everything that falls outside of the line.

Be particularly careful when tweezing the narrowest outer part of the brow. Look at where the root of the hair is—and exactly where the hair lies— to make sure that you won't be creating a gap by tweezing it.

Brush with success

Maintaining a clean, confident smile is as easy as two plus two. Brush your teeth twice a day for at least two minutes each time. Morning and evening are the dentists' recommended times. Two minutes is just the right amount of brushing needed to get at all of the teeth's curves and crevices, without wearing away tooth enamel—teeth will look and feel their sparkling best. Flossing daily is highly recommended. Using floss once a day, after you have brushed, is an excellent way to keep bacteria, gum disease, and tooth decay at bay.

Remember, a great smile is a beauty maker—and your teeth play one of the most important parts in making that smile so attractive. Take care of your teeth and your smile will beam!

Sum things up

How we age is dependent upon two factors: lifestyle and genes. While you can't change your parents, you can change your lifestyle. Take a look at some "age adders" and do the math.

⁕ Big city living: add five years to your age. Big cities have more vehicles and places for dirt and grime to hide. Be sure to compensate by using creams with more antioxidants in them. Adjust your supplements to reflect higher amounts of antioxidants as well.

⁕ Crash dieting: add ten years. Most of us have done it, but to keep doing it is the surest way to have skin that stretches and sags. Stick to a sensible eating plan—one that is good for life.

⁕ Sunbathing and tanning beds: add 20 years to your age. There is no bronze goddess—honest. The UVA and UVB damage is something that cannot be repaired—period.

⁕ Smoking: add 20 plus years to your age—your life, however, will be tragically cut short. Don't do it.

Chapter 5

Handle with care

Steamed up

Begin the facial cleansing process as the top spas do. Before cleaning the skin, soak a hand towel in a bowl of very warm water that has been infused with a chamomile tea bag. Soak the towel, ring out, and apply to the face and neck. Relax and allow the towel to cool. Chamomile is soothing to the skin and the steam from the towel opens up the pores, loosens up dead skin cells, and allows the cleanser to work more effectively. After the towel becomes cool, remove, cleanse skin as usual, tone, and apply moisturizer.

Inside/out

Swiss Kriss is a herbal laxative found at your local health food store. In addition to its inside-cleansing abilities, Swiss Kriss is also an excellent product to deep cleanse skin using a facial steam treatment. Bring a large pot of water to a boil. Remove from heat. Mix two tablespoons of Swiss Kriss into water. Allow to infuse for five minutes. With a large towel over your head, place your face over the steam, turning from side to side to deep steam all parts of the face. Be sure to keep your face at a far enough distance from the steam, yet close enough to enjoy all the herbal benefits. This wonderful mixture detoxifies the skin—the steam opens the pores and allows toxins to be released. Rinse the face in slightly cool water, pat dry, and end with a deep hydrating moisturizer.

Steps to beautiful skin

A skincare regime used twice a day will produce superior results compared to anything a professional spa can do on even a monthly basis. Properly cleansing, toning, exfoliating, and hydrating twice daily, combined with regularly scheduled spa visits, will produce the best skin possible.

Take it to the max

To optimize moisturizers and get the maximum benefits from the replenishing product, start with cleansed and toned skin. Gently apply a dime-sized dab to your skin. Using upward, circular motions, lightly massage the moisturizer into the face. If your skin is dry, massage until the product is absorbed. If your skin is oily, do not over-massage; it will stimulate the oil glands to produce more sebum—which is the last thing you need.

Leave the eye area open. Use an eye cream made especially for the delicate skin around the eyes. A regular moisturizer has the tendency to add puff to the eye area.

Moisturizers work by placing a barrier between the skin and the outside world and by pulling water from the air and delivering it to the surface of the skin.

Relax not extract

Resist the temptation to extract the occasional blackhead or whitehead yourself. You will spread the contents back into the skin, causing the surrounding oil gland to spread the infection. Plus you can permanently enlarge a pore—we have all seen it—don't do it. Make an appointment with an esthetician to have it removed properly, and schedule a deep cleansing facial while you are at it.

Don't stop

Don't forget that the skin doesn't stop at the chin line. You must apply all facial products to the neck and décolleté. These are two of the very first places to show signs of aging. It only takes a few extra seconds to possibly take away years—continue the skin care all the way down!

Black and white

Acne usually begins with a blackhead or whitehead. Blackheads are trapped pores filled with oil, dead cells, and dirt. It is called a blackhead because the area is exposed to air. A whitehead, which a blackhead can turn into, is when the area is completely sealed underneath the skin.

Acne can appear at any time throughout life. Skin with over-productive oil glands and large pores is most likely to experience some form of acne. Adult acne usually appears on the face, neck, shoulders, and back. Warmer seasons can contribute to breakouts. To keep acne at bay, keep the areas as clean as possible. Schedule a professional treatment to deeply cleanse your skin, extract dirt from the pores, and also to get advice on the most effective skincare regime for you. This is one condition you don't want to home remedy. Seek professional help.

Light handed

High-tech skincare products are meant
to be used in moderate amounts. Using
excess anything—cleansers, toners,
moisturizers, and other creams and
lotions—will not make your skin
younger, firmer, or more beautiful.
The skin can only absorb so much
at one time, so using the recommended
amount will produce much better results
than slathering it on like it's the fountain of youth.

Besides, excess cream that fails to penetrate could cause breakouts, as
well as spotty makeup application. Use good products, but use them well.

Cherry jubilee

Cherries are great for speeding up cell removal and also for exfoliating dead skin cells. This is due to the high content of malic acid found in cherries. Malic acid is one of the fruit acids used in multi-fruit acid professional treatments. Make your own at-home version of this spa treatment by mixing three tablespoons of pure cherry juice with two tablespoons of uncooked dry oatmeal. Spread evenly over the face and neck. Allow this mix to stay on the face for five to seven minutes. Gently rub the skin as you remove the mixture to encourage even more exfoliation. Rinse well and pat dry. Add your favorite moisturizer and you are all set with skin that is renewed and radiant. After all, cherry picking means getting the very best of all of the choices.

Choose from column A, B, C

Choose your skin care like an order from a Chinese menu. If company "A" has the perfect cleanser, then use it. If company "B" offers a night treatment that is best for your skin, order it. In spite of what the companies try to tell you, you do not need a particular company's entire line. Find products that suit your skin and your wallet—and don't be afraid to mix and match items to find the perfect combination for your face.

True grit

When it is time to use an exfoliator—be gentle. Let the product do the work. After cleansing the skin, take the exfoliating product and put a small amount onto a wet hand. Wet the other hand and gently go in circular motions around the face, neck, and décolleté. No pressure is needed since the product contains ingredients to lift the dead skin cells and debris from the skin. Rinse, rinse, rinse, with warm then cool water. Pat dry, and apply moisturizer.

On the web

Spider veins can appear on the face without prior notice. In most cases spider veins tend to go hand in hand with a porcelain complexion, simply because they are more visible on light skin.

One way to minimize the appearance of pesky spider veins is to keep temperatures even. Avoid extreme hot or cold as much as possible. Avoid steam rooms or saunas, and keep home central heating at a moderate level. Spicy foods and alcohol can also trigger an outbreak, so tread lightly. Vitamin K has been shown to help strengthen vein walls. Vitamin K is found in some moisturizers and can also be taken orally.

All for one

While some cosmetic companies insist on different cleansers for the eyes and face, this is simply not true. Eye makeup can easily be removed with your facial cleanser provided that the facial cleanser is gentle and non-irritating. Any cleanser has to work the hardest on mascara. Regular and water resistant (the only mascara you should be wearing anyway!) are water-based and will come off with your facial cleanser.

Waterproof mascara (not good to use at anytime!) contains higher amounts of wax, shellacs, or acrylates, and will require a mineral oil-based remover.

Keep the mascara resistant—not waterproof—and you can refrain from using two cleansers when one will do.

Deny the dry

For dewy skin, even in the dead of winter, keep a humidifier in your bedroom while you sleep. Before slipping under the sheets, slather on a bit of extra moisture, turn on the humidifier, and awaken with soft, hydrated skin.

Not my type

All skin has a type. Here is a guide to determine yours:

* Dry skin: feels tight and rough to the touch; dry patches often appear on skin's surface.

* Very dry skin or sensitive: prone to tightness and discomfort and is very sensitive. A lot of skincare products cause a reaction and irritate the skin.

* Combination skin: both oily and dry at the same time. Usually the forehead, nose, and chin are oily and shiny, prone to breakouts, blemishes, enlarged pores, and a never-ending shine.

Toner tip

Cotton pads and balls soak up liquids, like toner, all too quickly. Dampen the cotton with water first and squeeze out excess before putting toner on the cotton. You will use less product. This tip is excellent for sensitive skins, since toner can sometimes tingle.

Head to toe

Beautiful handbag. Fantastic shoes. Incredible designer clothes. All of them will never cover up neglected skin. Did you know that some people take better care of a silk blouse than they do of their own skin? Enjoy the couture, but take care of your face.

Tone up

A toner's job is to remove any excess cleanser from the skin as well as to ensure that the skin is toned and ready for the next treatment product. In addition to closing the skin's pores and removing excess cleansing product, a toner also helps to gently exfoliate extra dead skin cells.

Not toning the face is like washing the clothes without going through the rinse cycle. The rinse cycle removes excess cleanser. When selecting a toner, choose one that adds additional nutrients to the skin, such as vitamins and hydrators.

For those with sensitive facial skin, it is best to purchase a toner that is alcohol-free, to avoid aggravating your complexion. Even when you are in a hurry, there is no longer any excuse for not toning your skin—nowadays there are a great number of handy cleansing wipes on the market that combine cleansing and toning properties in one clean sweep. There are no excuses—get toning!

Night and day

While daytime moisturizers can pull double duty as night cream for some skins (normal or oily), night creams should not be used to do the day shift. Night creams are much thicker and heavier, and for good reason—their mission is to maximize protection over the course of the night and rehydrate the skin thoroughly while it is resting. While this is excellent for the vital P.M. skin renewal and repair, the thicker night cream will be too much under makeup, causing it to smear and smudge. Night creams used during the daytime may even cause breakouts, because they are not as readily absorbed into the skin and your pores will become clogged. In addition, nighttime varieties are not formulated with any form of sun protection, and, therefore, they are not as effective a barrier against the sun's rays.

Clean up your act

It is vital to always wash your hands before you begin to remove makeup, moisturize your skin, or touch your face in any way. Our hands are constantly exposed to all kinds of bacteria and germs. If you skip hand cleansing, you are mixing both dirt and grime into the skin as well as into the products you are using. From then on, every time you use that product you will be transferring bacteria to your face—counterproductive, don't you think?

Susie Galvez

Armed with quick wit, years of professional experience, and more get-pretty tips than a beauty pageant coordinator, expert makeup artist, esthetician, and author Susie Galvez is dedicated to giving women tools to help them accept themselves and realize that each day is another chance to be beautiful.

Inspired by the thrill she gets from helping women rediscover beauty on a daily basis, Susie wrote the *Ooh La La! Effortless Beauty* series which includes *Ooh La La! Perfect Face*, *Ooh La La! Perfect Body*, *Ooh La La! Perfect Makeup*, and *Ooh La La! Perfect Hair*.

Susie is also the author of *Hello Beautiful: 365 Ways to Be Even More Beautiful*, *Weight Loss Wisdom: 365 Successful Dieting Tips*, and *InSPArations: Ideas, tips & techniques to increase employee loyalty, client satisfaction and bottom-line spa profits*.

In addition to writing, Susie owns Face Works Day Spa in Richmond, Virginia. Face Works Day Spa has been featured in national and consumer magazines such as *Allure*, *Cosmopolitan*, *Elle*, and *Town and Country* as well as many trade publications including *Skin, Inc.*, *Dermascope*, *Day Spa*, *Salon Today*, *Nails*

Plus, *Nails*, *Spa Management*, and *Les Nouvelles Esthetiques*. In April 2002, The Day Spa Association recognized Face Works as one of only 12 fully accredited day spas—out of 1,000 members—in the United States.

Susie is also recognized as one of the leading consultants in the spa industry, and is in high demand as a speaker at international spa conventions. She is a featured spokesperson for the beauty industry on radio and television programs, and is a member of Cosmetic Executive Women, The National Association of Women Business Owners, and the Society of American Cosmetic Chemists.

You can contact Susie at www.susiegalvez.com or by visiting her beauty website at www.beautyatyourfingertips.com, where you will find even more ways to have Ooh La La moments! Be sure to sign up for your free spa-at-home tips!

Special appreciation

"Follow your bliss." Joseph Campbell

This book could not have been completed without the unwavering support and love of my very special friends. Thank you for allowing me to follow my bliss:

To my Aunt Esther for introducing me to the fun of taking care of my skin.

Audra Baca whose youthful spirit and turn of the word captured "me" on paper.

Dottie Dehart and Celia Rocks for their persistence in carrying my message out to the multitudes day after day.

Zaro Weil, friend and publisher, who entrusted me with her title.

To the superb esthetician staff at Face Works Day Spa, who are responsible for creating perfect faces for our clients, Sarah Ruben, Windi Baker, Celeste Ross, and Brandy Bittner.

And lastly, but always first with me, thank you Tino Galvez who is truly the wind beneath my wings.

XOXO